Hare Kṛṣṇa

Hare Kṛṣṇa

Kṛṣṇa Kṛṣṇa

Hare Hare

Hare Rāma

Hare Rāma

Rāma Rāma

Hare Hare

Published by
GOLOKA EDUCATION PVT. LTD.

URL: www.golokaeducation.com
Email: info@golokaeducation.com

All quotes & images of
His Divine Grace A.C. Bhaktivedanta Swami Prabhupada
are used with permission from
The Bhaktivedanta Book Trust International © 2018

Graphics by freepik.com

ISBN – 978-1-073647-972

Also by Mahatma Das
Uplift Yourself, Change the World
Living the Wisdom of Bhakti

Japa

AFFIRMATIONS
by Mahatma Das

His Divine Grace A.C. Bhaktivedanta Swami Prabhupāda

Dedication

This book is dedicated to my spiritual master, His Divine Grace A.C. Bhaktivedanta Swami Prabhupāda, ISKCON Founder-Ācārya, without whom we would not have had the fortune to taste the nectar of the holy name.

I also dedicate this book to all the devotees who are anxious to improve their *japa* and taste the sweetness of the *mahā-mantra*. I pray it helps them make chanting their rounds their favorite activity.

And lastly, this book is dedicated to all the devotees who have attended (and will attend in the future) my *Japa Workshop*. These affirmations are based on the essential principles of that workshop.

Japa Affirmations

Japa Affirmations

Japa Affirmations

Audio rendition of above affirmations can be found at

https://soundcloud.com/mahatma-das/japa-affirmations-and-explanations

Introduction

This handbook summarizes, in the form of affirmations, the main teachings, practices and attitudes I offer in my *Japa Workshops*. The explanations of these affirmations have been transcribed from a talk from one of these workshops.

The insights and attitudes contained within these affirmations have helped many devotees improve their chanting. Some devotees have even found that these affirmations have transformed their *japa*.

It is my hope that the mood these affirmations create will enable us to deeply relish our daily *japa*.

Your servant,
Mahatma Das

Mahatma Das

1.
I happily and enthusiastically welcome the holy names every japa session.

This first affirmation is meant to set the proper mood for *japa*. Sometimes devotees who haven't had the best experiences with *japa*, begin chanting in a negative mood, reasoning that since their *japa* hasn't been good in general, it will be the same again today. Thus, they begin *japa* with an expectation of a negative experience, approaching it more as a chore than a loving relationship.

This first affirmation is meant to create the mood one has when welcoming a very special guest. The holy name is our guest and we are welcoming Him to our home. We make our home and heart attractive because we want to make the time with our guest special, and we want Him to feel happy in our home. We thus adjust our consciousness in preparation for and anticipation of a special *japa* session.

To prepare for *japa* some devotees will read verses or prayers about the holy name, some will take a moment to reflect on the meaning of the *mantra* and some will focus on their intentions for their *japa* session. This is to place themselves in a positive, welcoming state in relation to the holy name. The main idea of the first affirmation is to get ourselves in the right state of mind for *japa*.

We prepare ourselves before chanting in order to ensure that we chant mindfully. Rather than thinking the goal of *japa* is to somehow or other just finish our prescribed number of rounds, we shift our consciousness into a different attitude: we view chanting as an exciting opportunity to connect with the Lord, something that we enthusiastically look forward to.

2.

I easily chant my prescribed number of rounds with focus and attention.

Affirmations prepare us to enter a task with a positive and favorable attitude. Many people ask whether we can easily chant with focus and attention just by affirming we will chant this way. While it may seem simplistic to believe that an affirmation can improve our *japa*, consider, for example, how believing we can't chant with focus and attention affects us. It creates a self-fulfilling prophecy, and thus we find it difficult to focus. After all, why would we try to focus if we believe we can't? This problem is exacerbated when we continue to chant daily with a lack of attention and focus. We then expect our *japa* to always be more or less like this. Thus, the belief that we can't focus well becomes the cause of not focusing. And continuing to chant without focus strengthens the belief that we can't focus. It then becomes a vicious cycle. So, just as a negative affirmation works against us, positive affirmations work for us by aligning our attitude with our goal of good *japa*.

Attention is an interesting phenomenon. Our mind has many thoughts, not only bad thoughts. So controlling our mind really means controlling our attention. For example, right now we can place our attention on Vṛndāvana or we can place our attention on other things. Since we do have control of our attention, this affirmation is meant to remind us that placing our attention on the holy names is not difficult if we set out to do this. The idea is that when we begin our *japa* session we shouldn't expect it to be a struggle. Rather, we alter our attitude to think that giving attention to the holy names is natural. We want to create a mood in which we feel it's natural and easy to chant with focus and attention, not that it is some herculean task that only a few people can accomplish. Also, if we consider *japa* to be essentially important to our spiritual life, then it's going to be much easier to chant with attention since we naturally give attention to what's most important in our lives. With this affirmation we confirm that it is possible to be attentive, and that we will control our attention while chanting.

3.

When I chant, I chant.

Although this affirmation sounds simplistic, it is actually quite profound. When we chant, we often are disconnected from the holy name, being either externally or internally distracted from our chanting. "When I chant, I chant" encompasses the principle behind everything I teach in *The Japa Workshop*. When we chant, our whole world should be put on hold. It must be about us and Kṛṣṇa, and nothing else. Sometimes I joke that the 11th offense is to have our cellphone on when we are chanting. In other words, when we chant we shouldn't be doing anything else: we should not be on our computer, reading a book, or doing this or that. We should just be with the holy name.

Once we clear all external distractions, we must also internally stop thinking about doing anything else. Some devotees say that when they chant they give their time totally to the holy name free of all external distractions. They chant in a quiet place (we call this chanting in our "sacred space"), but when asked if they have also created an internal sacred space, often the answer is no. "When I chant, I chant" means not only creating the external space, but more importantly creating the internal environment in which we don't allow ourselves to be distracted. We could also say, "When I study, I study," or "When I work, I work" because it is the same principle. For example, I have seen people become so absorbed in reading their newspaper that they become oblivious to everything around them. We should be this way with our *japa*. When we chant, we want to be completely given over to our *japa* and not to anything else, either externally or internally.

4.
I get to chant, I want to chant, and I love to chant.

Often, when we begin our *japa*, we don't feel inspired to chant. We would rather be doing something else, or we feel that it's going to be difficult or boring to chant, fearing we won't be able to control our mind. In other words, we may fear that our *japa* session is going to be a struggle. If our chanting is not generally good, or has not been good recently, these thoughts are likely to haunt us. We may not even realize we are thinking this way, but before beginning *japa* notice if there is a subtle voice that sometimes says, "Oh no, here we go again." Now we might say, "I do feel this way sometimes, but how is saying, 'I get to chant, I want to chant and I love to chant' going to make a difference?"

My belief is that fundamentally we do love to chant, we do want to chant, and we do view *japa* as a special blessing. In the many workshops I have done, I have asked devotees, "What would your life be like without the holy name? What if you were prevented from chanting? How would you feel?" When asked these questions everyone says, "That would be horrible." This means at heart we all want to chant, we appreciate the holy names, and we see chanting as an opportunity rather than a burden. So, on a deep level we do want to chant. We made a commitment to chant. No one forced us. We wanted to become purified and closer to Kṛṣṇa.

When we chant properly, we love chanting. And we love the effects of chanting even when chanting is difficult. Connect to the holy names on this level. Realize that we really do "want to chant, get to chant and love to chant," even if we don't always consciously feel that way. This affirmation can connect us with our natural desire to chant. Many devotees have told me that just saying this affirmation before they begin chanting has a tremendously positively effect on their *japa*. I know it might sound strange that a few words could make that kind of difference. But they are not just saying the words; they are connecting with their desire to chant and bringing their conscious mind to this awareness. This affirmation will remind us that we really do appreciate chanting. Just by saying, "I get to chant, I want to chant, and I love to chant" we alter our attitude towards the holy name, and thus alter our experience.

In addition to beginning our *japa* with this affirmation, if we are losing our connection, or are getting bored or distracted while chanting, then this affirmation is a very powerful way to reconnect to the holy names. It's a reminder of how important *japa* is to us. As we cite this affirmation, we affirm to ourselves that we appreciate the holy name and the rare opportunity we have to chant.

5.

I treat the maha-mantra as Radha and Kṛṣṇa, fully present in sound.

Śrīla Prabhupāda said that intellectually we cannot understand that the holy name is non-different from Kṛṣṇa; it is something that we must experience. Those of us from the West did not understand the concept of God being present in a deity, for example, but with faith in Prabhupāda's words we worshipped the deity as Kṛṣṇa. Because we worshipped the deity with that kind of faith, we began to realize and experience that Kṛṣṇa is indeed non-different from the deity. We experienced His presence and we became attached to the deity.

It's the same with the holy name. We may not be able to intellectually understand how Kṛṣṇa is the same as His name, but we can experience it. This affirmation will get us off the intellectual platform and help us embrace the name as Kṛṣṇa. We may not always have much of an experience of Kṛṣṇa in His name, but when we place awareness on the reality that we are associating with Rādhā and Kṛṣṇa while we chant, our experience of Kṛṣṇa in His name deepens. When we worship the deity in this same consciousness, we begin to experience the presence, mercy, and various aspects of our relationship with the deity. In the same way, when we treat the holy name as Rādhā and Kṛṣṇa deities in the form of sound, we increasingly experience and realize the presence of Rādhā and Kṛṣṇa in Their names.

Prabhupāda said the name is non-different from Kṛṣṇa, that Kṛṣṇa is fully present in His name. Therefore, we affirm that we will treat the holy name as Kṛṣṇa, fully present in sound. We bow down to the holy name within our heart, and we chant the holy name with the understanding that this is Kṛṣṇa. Śrīla Prabhupāda once said when we chant the holy name it's the same as taking darshan of the deities. When the curtains open, we bow down. Similarly, we should bow down to the holy name as we chant, thinking that Kṛṣṇa is manifesting His presence before us.

6.

I receive and feel Kṛṣṇa's presence, mercy and love in His holy names.

When we allow ourselves to feel Kṛṣṇa in His name, or feel the mercy coming to us through His name, we put ourselves in a "receiver's mood." An achiever's mood means we are trying to squeeze something from the name as opposed to receiving what's already coming to us through the name (the mercy, love, and blessings in the name). It's an awareness that what we are trying to get from the holy name already exists within it. We don't struggle to feel the mercy, bliss and nectar of the name; rather we are allowing ourselves to bathe in the mercy, bliss and nectar that already exists within the name. It is just like when we are given something; we don't have to create it, we only have to put our hands out, accept it and enjoy its benefits.

This affirmation is meant to put us in the consciousness that rather than making the holy name bless us, we are simply trying to appreciate the blessings already in the name and how they are coming to us as we chant. If I say I love and appreciate you, you feel my love. The holy name is saying, "I am present here, my mercy is here, my love is here, please accept it, please feel it, please utilize it."

7.
I chant in full awareness that the holy name is my greatest treasure.

This is similar to the last affirmation and is based on the *Harināma Cintāmaṇi*. The holy name is the greatest jewel in the Lord's treasury because the holy name awakens our love for Kṛṣṇa and this love is our greatest wealth. At the same time, to have a relationship with us is one of Kṛṣṇa's most cherished desires. Although He has everything, He doesn't have our heart and He hankers for it – and is anxiously waiting for us to return to Him. And since the *mahā-mantra* will cause us to give our heart to Kṛṣṇa, He will get from us what He most desires through the *mahā-mantra*.

The holy name not only gives us the strength we need to continue in Kṛṣṇa consciousness, but also fully reveals our eternal form, relationship and service. Plus, without the holy names there would be no possibility of achieving

Kṛṣṇa consciousness in the mood of the residents of Vṛndāvana. The *mahā-mantra* is thus Kṛṣṇa offering us a relationship with Him. If we chant His name without offense, we will revive that relationship and we will please Kṛṣṇa. What could be more valuable than this?

8.

I chant to please Radha and Kṛṣṇa, not to gain anything material.

It is said that if we chant the holy name to receive something material, or with the intention of making material progress, it is an offense to the holy name. The very mood, the very essence, the very meaning that the vibration carries is, "I want pure devotional service." If we hear the holy name speaking to us, He is saying that surrender is the most relishable and desirable position. The holy names, when chanted properly, naturally inspire our desire for pure devotional service. Therefore, if we are chanting the holy names but are not in this mood, we are out of alignment with the holy names. If while chanting we are asking Kṛṣṇa to fulfill our material desires rather than connecting to the pure mood of the holy names, then this is impure *bhakti*. For example, *māyāvadis* use the holy names to merge into the *brahmajyoti* or *sahajiyās* use Kṛṣṇa to fulfill their material desires. We chant the holy name only to further develop the attitude of unmotivated service (service whose only motivation is to please Kṛṣṇa).

This affirmation is a reminder that we don't chant to try to become materially happy. Of course, in the beginning we may have been motivated to chant to gain something for ourselves. But pure chanting requires that our only motive is to purify our heart, to please Kṛṣṇa and to develop our love for Him.

If our chanting becomes mechanical, we can remember this affirmation: "I chant to please Rādhā and Kṛṣṇa." We may even wish to imagine Kṛṣṇa is with us (in His holy name) and He is enjoying hearing us chant and seeing us becoming purified. He also enjoys seeing our determination to continue to chant enthusiastically even when we are not tasting the holy names. He wants to see what we will do during these times. Will we give up, allow ourselves to get distracted, or continue with enthusiasm, determination and a desire to please Him, even when we are not experiencing a taste? The paradox is that if we are not experiencing a taste, just by chanting to please Kṛṣṇa we will experience a taste.

9.

I am out of my mind and in my heart, fully present to the holy names when I chant.

To say "you are out of your mind" is another way of saying you are crazy. We use this humor to explain that if we are in our mind when we chant, it means we are not present to the holy names. Whereas if we are in our heart, we are present to the experience of the holy name. For example, some feel Kṛṣṇa's presence in the vibration of His names within their body. Others feel His presence in the vibration of the holy names they feel around them. Whatever the case, Prabhupāda stated that we can feel Kṛṣṇa when we chant.

This affirmation helps us understand more deeply Prabhupāda's statement, "Where is the question of the mind?" which was his response to the statement, "It is very difficult to control my mind when I chant." He elaborated, "You just chant with your tongue and hear with your ear." (Morning Walk, February 1975, Honolulu, Hawaii) In other words, the mind is not required for hearing and experiencing the holy name; in fact it is the mind that takes us away from experiencing the holy name when it focuses on the past or future.

When I say I am out of my mind and in my heart, it also means that I am expressing my spiritual desires to Kṛṣṇa while chanting, rather than thinking of things not related to chanting. Prabhupāda once said that when we chant Kṛṣṇa comes to us and says, "Yes, what do you want?" So, while chanting we express our desire to Kṛṣṇa. "I want purity; I want to overcome my *anarthas*; I want to be empowered; I want to be free from anything that is destructive to my relationship; etc." In this way we pray from our heart through the *mahā-mantra*.

While chanting we are not thinking of our prayers as much as we are feeling our prayers. If we are thinking more than feeling, then we are still in our mind ("Where is the question of the mind?"). For example, if we meet someone we sense isn't trustworthy, it comes more as a feeling that we can't trust them than a thought. In fact, the thought comes after the feeling. Similarly, when we are praying while chanting, we are feeling, "Kṛṣṇa please help me; please bring me closer to you; please make me pure," not thinking these things. Prayer is not a thought process. The more we feel, the more we get out of our mind and into our heart.

Praying to – and through – the holy name is a powerful way to control our mind and absorb ourselves in the holy name. Some devotees wonder: "If I try to enter into feeling, then won't it take my focus off hearing the name?" The two are not separate processes. Hearing and praying are one, and when we experience this oneness, we realize that by praying we become more absorbed in hearing (it's a holistic experience).

What we chant with our lips is one thing, but what we feel is what really communicates. Śrīla Bhaktisiddhānta Sarasvatī Ṭhākura said we don't chant with our lips, we chant with our heart. Feeling is the essence of prayer, and feeling brings us into the present. So feeling can absorb us completely in chanting. The idea of this affirmation is that we are not just chanting with our tongue, but we are chanting with our heart. And remember, when we are out of our mind, we are in our heart.

10.
I fully honor my sacred relationship with the holy names during japa.

Chanting is a relationship and we make a mistake when we see it only as a process. Of course, chanting is one of the nine processes of devotional service, but it is a mistake to treat chanting in a ritualistic way, as if the essence of chanting is to perfectly follow a specific set of external rituals, rules, or standards.

When chanting *japa* (or learning how to chant *japa*), it is common to try to understand *japa* in a more process-oriented or mechanical way. How should we sit? What direction should we face? Is it okay to stand or walk? How do we pronounce the *mantra* perfectly? What is the ideal amount of time it should take to chant each round? These considerations are more mechanical or external. They can, of course, be helpful, but they can also distract us from the deeper mood of chanting if they become our main focus. If we focus too much on the mechanical side, thinking that the goal is to perfect the mechanics of *japa*, then we can lose touch with the reality that we have a relationship with the holy name, not with a process, and that this relationship continues to develop as we continue to chant.

This affirmation is encouraging us to go deeper than the external process of chanting, to realize that chanting, although a process, is essentially a relationship.

11.

I chant to be accepted by Kṛṣṇa and to repair my broken relationship with Him.

Prabhupāda gave the following definition of the *mahā-mantra* in 1968: "Kṛṣṇa, please accept me, please accept me." Interestingly, in a later lecture he said we have no right to ask Kṛṣṇa to accept us. We have no right because we left Him; we turned our back on Him; we committed sinful activities for many, many lifetimes. We became envious of Kṛṣṇa, we denied Him, and we minimized Him. What right do we have now to ask Him to accept us? Our desire to reconnect with Kṛṣṇa is our great fortune. As such, we cannot stop ourselves from asking Kṛṣṇa to accept us. Prabhupāda said, "We have faith in our Guru Mahārāja and we know by his mercy he will petition Kṛṣṇa and Kṛṣṇa will accept us." It is powerful to chant in the mood that "We have turned our back on Kṛṣṇa, we have remained separated from Him for many, many lifetimes and now we are asking Him,

'Please, although I don't deserve it, I want to reinstate my relationship with you. Please accept me.'"

If we allow ourselves to enter into this mood, it will likely bring up emotions like remorse, despair and lamentation. But these feelings can empower our chanting. Feeling guilty for having left Kṛṣṇa, and feeling the need to reconnect, will energize our *japa*.

In this meditation we can envision the example that Prabhupāda gave of a child who has run away from home. Although the parents love him, the child wants independence and therefore leaves home. I like to envision myself as this child coming back years later as an adult (lifetimes later) to my father (Kṛṣṇa) having suffered much. Realizing my mistakes, I am ready to humbly plead to Kṛṣṇa to accept me back. I envision myself knocking on Kṛṣṇa's door preparing to ask Him to forgive me and accept me, even though I have turned my back on Him. I know I don't deserve the relationship, so I can only beg to be accepted. I feel bad, I feel guilty, I feel horrible, yet I need to be accepted – and thus I beg for it. If we bring out these emotions while chanting, we enter a deeply prayerful realm of *japa*.

12.
I chant from my heart, feelingly praying to come closer to Kṛṣṇa.

As mentioned before, Śrīla Bhaktisiddhānta Sarasvatī Ṭhākura said that we don't chant with our lips, we chant with our heart. The exact words are, "The holy name is not lip deep; it's heart deep." Although people may say loving things, what's expressed from their heart is what actually communicates their love. It is important to be aware that as we are chanting a *mantra* which means "Kṛṣṇa, please engage me in your service," "Kṛṣṇa, please accept me," "Kṛṣṇa, bring me closer to you," if we are not feeling this way while chanting, we might be feeling something like, "I don't like chanting," or, "I vowed to chant 16 rounds and I am just doing my duty and trying to get my rounds done as quickly as possible." Or we may be meditating on how difficult it is to focus our mind, how hard it is to complete our 16 rounds, or even how much we don't feel like chanting. In doing so, we disconnect from the feeling/meaning of the *mantra*. The *mahā-mantra* is a prayer to come closer to Kṛṣṇa, so we always want to be in that mood when chanting. We want to communicate from the heart, not from the lips. Chanting which is only from the lips is compared to shooting a blank bullet. A blank bullet is not actually a bullet, but it makes an explosion like a bullet. Similarly, we can be chanting blank *mantras*, *mantras* without substance that only sound like the *mahā-mantra*. And we cannot defeat *māyā* by shooting blank *mantras*. You might question, "But I thought Kṛṣṇa was in His name?" He is, just as the deity is Kṛṣṇa. But we may not see the deity as Kṛṣṇa due to our mentality. In the same way, we may not realize Kṛṣṇa in His name due to improper chanting. In fact, Śrīla Bhaktisiddhānta said Kṛṣṇa is not in His name but descends in His name when we chant with a service attitude.

We have experience of this. When we chant improperly we don't feel that we have just spent two hours with Kṛṣṇa. We don't really feel spiritually enlivened. We might even feel relieved to have finished our rounds. If we don't feel a connection with or purification from the holy name, we can ask ourselves, "Was I actually chanting the holy name or was I just making a sound?" "Was there any substance to my chanting?" To chant from the heart, feelingly praying to come closer to Kṛṣṇa is what the *mahā-mantra* means. If we could translate the feeling of the *mahā-mantra* into words, it would say, "Kṛṣṇa, I want to come closer to you, I want to serve you, I want to be pure." We want to connect deeply with what the holy name means. We want to be connected on the same frequency that the holy name vibrates.

13.
I meditate on the meaning of the holy names as I chant.

Our *ācāryas* have given us many meanings for the holy name, and each meaning contains deep emotions. "Kṛṣṇa, make me qualified to serve you," "Kṛṣṇa, bring my heart closer to you," "Kṛṣṇa, please accept me," "Kṛṣṇa, please purify me," "Kṛṣṇa, uplift me." So when we say "I meditate on the meanings," it means we are conscious, on an emotional level, of what the *mahā-mantra* means. We don't chant in a blank, feelingless state; we chant while meditating on – and feeling – the meaning of the *mantra*.

Sometimes when we chant, we text a little bit, maybe talk with someone or perhaps get distracted by something. This affirmation is encouraging us to avoid such distractions. Meditating on the meaning of the holy name isn't possible if we chant and look at our phone, chant and talk to our friends, etc. I call this "Chat and be happy." But chatting Hare Kṛṣṇa is not the same as chanting Hare Kṛṣṇa!

When we enter more deeply into the holy name, we align emotionally with the meanings of the name. For example, let's say someone is talking to us about something serious and we're just smiling. This is inappropriate because we are out of sync with the mood of the conversation. In the same way, if we are not connected to the meanings of the holy name then we are out of alignment with the nature and frequency of the *mahā-mantra*.

The holy name's meanings are deep, profound and emotional, but if we just mumble through the *mantra* then we are likely not connecting properly with the holy names. To test yourselves, record your chanting for a few minutes. Don't try to perform for the recording; just chant as you normally do. Then play back the recording and listen to your mood. What feeling is your chanting conveying (devotion, boredom, excitement, botheration, apathy)?

This affirmation is especially useful when we feel disconnected from the vibration of the holy name, because it helps us enter into the emotions contained in the various meanings of the *mantra*.

To enter this mood we can ask ourselves, "Why am I chanting?" In other words, we check in while chanting and ask ourselves, "What does this chanting mean?" "What am I trying to accomplish?" "What is the goal of *japa*?" This will bring our consciousness and heart in alignment – on an emotional level – with the meanings of the holy names.

14.

I turn off my world and turn on Kṛṣṇa's world when I chant my rounds.

As mentioned before, when we are chanting we may sometimes be thinking about what's going on in our life. We might think about what we have to do, things we like and don't like, problems to deal with, etc. Whatever the case, such thoughts are about our life, not Kṛṣṇa's life. (This is interesting because the holy name includes Kṛṣṇa's *līlās*, not our *līlās*.)

I am often asked, "How can I control my mind while chanting?" One of the reasons our mind wanders is that we haven't told our mind, "While I am chanting you have a break. I am turning you off. In fact, I am turning my whole life off." So when we begin chanting we need to mentally turn off all the lights in our life. In other words, turn off the lights of what we didn't finish yesterday, what we have to do today, the problems we are facing, etc. When we don't do this, we give the mind license to think of these things while we chant. And this makes controlling the mind difficult.

It can also be helpful to internally create a *bhajan kutir*, an internal space in which our world is turned off and the only thing allowed in is Kṛṣṇa in the form of His holy name. Another thing that is helpful is to get up early and then create a "time free zone." This means to imagine that our day doesn't start until after *japa*. In other words, during the morning when we are chanting, we are mentally not in our day yet. So let's say our day begins at 7 am and we are up at 5 am. We remind ourselves that our day doesn't begin until 7 and thus there is nothing to think about during *japa* other than Kṛṣṇa. If we can get ourselves into this consciousness, we will find it much easier to focus.

And this is easier to do than we may think. We do this every night when we turn off our lives and go to sleep. We also do this when we turn off our world to watch a movie, surf the internet, read a book or engage in a hobby. This affirmation is meant to remind us to create the proper internal space before we begin chanting.

15.
I chant with no other motive than to render pure devotional service.

This sounds similar to the affirmation in which we state that we chant without asking for anything material. What's significant is that this is the main meaning Prabhupāda had given us for the holy name, i.e. Kṛṣṇa, please engage me in your service, which also means please engage me in pure service. Prabhupāda elaborated on this meaning in a lecture, which I am paraphrasing as: My dear Lord, for so long I have been engaged in *māyā's* service, now I want to engage only in your service; so please put me under the shelter of your internal potency and uplift me, pick me up, pull me away from *māyā*. I don't want to be her servant anymore, I just want to be the servant of you, of Rādhā, under Rādhā's energy, your internal potency.

Śrīla Bhaktisiddhānta Sarasvatī Ṭhākura used to say that when we are chanting we should be in a service mood.

The real holy name is the holy name which is imbued with this service mentality. As we mentioned before, Śrīla Bhaktisiddhānta said the holy name descends when we chant in this mood.

Because we are meant to be a servant of the holy name, we try to chant in a humble state of mind, not as an enjoyer of the holy name. I am a servant of the holy name, I am a servant of Kṛṣṇa, and I am chanting to awaken the pure mood of service. All we want is a pure serving attitude and pure serving emotion. This is the proper mood with which to chant.

16.

My beads are my connection with Kṛṣṇa and my ticket back to Godhead.

Śrīla Prabhupāda wrote to Girirāj Swami, "Your beads are your connection to Kṛṣṇa." Prabhupāda also said 16 rounds is your ticket back to Godhead. On one occasion he told Trivikrāma Swami that chanting is the essence of our philosophy. And he told Hansadutta Prabhu that the purpose of reading his books is to bring us to the stage of pure chanting. Still, we sometimes forget how important chanting is.

Obviously, *japa* is essentially important because it is the only activity we vow to do when we take initiation (we vow not to do four things, and vow to do one thing). In Kali-yuga chanting is the most important process in devotional service, so if we don't give priority to our chanting then our spiritual life will suffer. One of the purposes of the *Japa Retreats* and *Japa Workshops*

is to inspire devotees to give more importance to their *japa*. When we give more importance to our chanting, our chanting naturally improves. Sometimes we see that devotees go to a *Japa Workshop* but in a few weeks the importance they give to the holy name diminishes. Even though they learned much, they can easily revert to their former ways of chanting if they don't make *japa* a priority. This is because what we give importance to is what we do well.

If we don't give importance to our relationships, we probably won't have good relationships. If we don't give importance to earning money, we probably won't have much money. If we don't give importance to our health, we probably won't be in really good shape. And if we don't give importance to *japa*, our *japa* probably won't be very good. If we give more importance to our *japa*, it will naturally improve.

The purpose of this affirmation is to remind us, or make us aware, that *japa* is the most important activity of our day. Of all the rules and regulations given to us, Śrīla Prabhupāda said that chanting 16 rounds is the most essential. And all the other processes are contained within our *japa*. Thus *japa* is something we never want to minimize, something that must always be given the highest priority.

17.

I am totally dependent on guru and Kṛṣṇa to chant quality japa every day.

In *Harināma Cintāmaṇi*, Śrīla Bhaktivinoda Ṭhākura poses this question: "How can we overcome the offense of distraction?" He answers that we can't overcome it on our own; we need the mercy of guru and Kṛṣṇa. In other words, pure chanting is not achieved by our effort alone. Although we may implement strategies, tools and attitudes to improve our chanting, without mercy these alone will not make us successful.

This affirmation is meant to remind us that whatever success we have in chanting is a result of mercy. This doesn't mean that our efforts to improve our chanting are not required, because mercy comes in proportion to our effort. So, by implementing ways in which to improve our chanting, guru and Kṛṣṇa reciprocate by helping us in the areas we are endeavoring to improve.

Our efforts attract the mercy of guru and Kṛṣṇa, and thus improvements in *japa* happen by their mercy.

Act like everything depends on you but pray like everything depends on God.

18.

I organize my life to make japa the most important activity of my day.

If we don't consciously organize our life in a way that supports our *japa*, it's possible that aspects of our lifestyle may undermine good *japa*. For example, if we stay up late, we won't get up early. And rising late can negatively affect our *japa*. If we read a book or watch something not related to Kṛṣṇa, this too could have a negative effect on our *japa*. If we allow ourselves to be so busy that we have little or no time for reading, *pūjā*, or service, our chanting will tend to be more mechanical than heartfelt. And if we are critical of devotees, this will definitely be harmful to our Kṛṣṇa consciousness.

There are also things we can do that will enhance our *japa*. For example, giving the holy name to others, preaching and distributing books, and/or performing additional austerity or service empowers our chanting.

For those who work, if we are engaged in service in our spare time, rather than using our free time for activities not related to Kṛṣṇa, this will also help our chanting. And if we use our time to study the theology of the holy name, or read books and/or listen to lectures about improving *japa*, this will help us by keeping us focused on the need to chant well.

The idea of this affirmation is to look at our life and consider whether we are doing anything which is undermining our ability to chant well, and also look at what we can do in our life that would support better chanting. As we know, most of the ten offenses do not directly refer to chanting, but what we do when we are not chanting. Our lifestyle, attitudes, and activities affect our consciousness. Indeed, everything we see, say, hear, smell, taste, or do affects our consciousness. And our consciousness affects our chanting. This affirmation is meant to encourage us to organize our life in a way that supports good *japa*. As we become more conscious of how our activities affect our *japa*, we can make little changes in our life to help avoid anything that might negatively impact our *japa* and engage in activities that support good chanting. As such, this affirmation brings awareness of how our lifestyle may either be helping or harming our *japa*.

19.

I make excellent japa my standard and focus on continually improving.

One of the most important goals of *The Japa Workshop*, which this affirmation encourages, is to make bad *japa* unacceptable. In other words, we set a higher standard of *japa* for ourselves, and *japa* that falls below this standard becomes an unacceptable way of chanting for us.

Secondly, this affirmation is meant to help us always strive to improve the quality of our *japa*. The reason this affirmation is so important is that it addresses a problem many of us have: chanting poorly day in and day out without trying to improve ourselves. Even if we do endeavor to improve, there is often a fear that the improvement we make won't last and we'll fall back into our old *japa* habits. This affirmation is meant to encourage us to commit to not allowing ourselves to chant poor *japa* by creating an internal threshold that we will not allow ourselves to go below, and then gradually raise that threshold over time. If we commit to a higher standard of *japa* and deeply ingrain that standard within ourselves, then when we start to go below that standard we'll automatically correct ourselves. In this way, we can ensure that our *japa* will always be good. It's like a fuel gauge. As soon as we see our fuel gauge is nearing empty, we fill it up. Similarly, as soon as our *japa* level goes below "good" we immediately fill it up.

"I make excellent *japa* my standard" is meant to help us preserve better *japa* habits. Let us make both good *japa* and continual improvement our new standard. Let us never allow ourselves to chant anything but good rounds. If we can deeply imbibe this consciousness, i.e. bad *japa* is non-negotiable, the effects on the quality of our *japa* – and on our lives – will be significant.

20.
I relish chanting the holy names.

What is the importance of this affirmation? We want to always be in the consciousness that chanting is so sweet, so precious, and so special that we are unlimitedly grateful to be blessed with the opportunity to chant. Although chanting becomes most relishable at the stage of *ruci* (taste) and beyond, we still want to be in the consciousness now that we are extremely fortunate to be chanting. This consciousness allows us to better appreciate the opportunity we have to chant the holy names daily, and as a consequence gain greater taste for chanting. You might ask whether we can relish chanting just by focusing on how much we appreciate the only name or simply by stating that we relish chanting our rounds. Of course, I can't guarantee that's always going to happen, but reminding ourselves that chanting is a special gift definitely helps create a more positive attitude towards *japa*.

In the higher stages of *bhakti*, we will always relish chanting the holy names. This affirmation is meant to remind us that we, the soul, certainly relish chanting. This is especially helpful to remember when we are not experiencing much of a taste during *japa*.

Conclusion

When we take a test, our performance is determined by how well we are prepared. In other words, present performance is a result of past preparation. *Japa* is much like this. The consciousness with which we approach our *japa* (this is going to be blissful, this is going to be difficult, I don't feel that I can concentrate well for 16 rounds, I will relish chanting, I won't relish chanting, etc.) has a huge effect on the quality of our *japa*. Proper consciousness can be evoked by the prayers and attitudes we bring to our *japa* in the moments before we begin our first round, and in the ways we think in general about what is possible, or not possible, to achieve with our *japa*.

In life, we rarely go higher than our highest thought. We also rarely go further in any endeavor than what we set out to achieve. This means that where we are looking to go (our goals and intentions) is much more important than where we presently stand. In terms of *japa*, this means what we are expecting/desiring/hoping to get from our *japa* in terms of the quality of our chanting and the experiences we get during *japa*, will greatly influence how much we are willing to improve our *japa*. Therefore, it is important for us to focus on where we want to go with our *japa*, rather than focus on our fears of the undesirable places we might land up in (those fears often stem from a belief that we can't always do what we know we should do). This is a problem we need to intelligently deal with because we desperately need to avoid being satisfied with poor or average *japa*. To not aspire after being absorbed in our rounds or to not have the intention to experience *japa* on a deeper level, will almost certainly guarantee that our *japa* remains the same – or gets worse. Fear is a belief in our inadequacy to deal with something. Doubt is a conflict between new decisions and old decisions.

Whether we realize it or not, much of the quality of our *japa* is a decision we made long ago about such things as what we can expect from *japa* (in terms of taste and realization), how well we can actually chant, or how Kṛṣṇa conscious we believe we can be. These decisions then become the deciding factor in how much effort we are willing to put into our *japa*. It's not uncommon for devotees to come to a point where they don't even try to improve their chanting much because they think, for these and other reasons, it is not possible to do much better.

If we are not satisfied with the quality of our *japa*, we should focus on the kind of *japa* we wish to create – and then act deliberately to create it. Of course, we can't just make things happen because we want them that way, but because Kṛṣṇa reciprocates with our desires to advance, our *japa* improves when we both want it to improve and make the effort to improve it. Man proposes and God disposes.

So what are you proposing for your *japa*? What you think of as impossible to achieve might actually be achievable if you think differently. I am suggesting that you think differently about what is possible for your *japa*. If we want to improve our *japa*, we can. How? We set our intentions on better *japa* – and act on those intentions. So one of two things will happen. We will either chant in ways we choose, or chant according to how our environment/conditioning/default *japa* settings dictate.

We can make the choice between our goals and our conditioning. Of course, the big question is what will we choose. The choice for increased quality *japa* will "give us a taste of the nectar for which we are always anxious" and continually nourish our Kṛṣṇa consciousness with inspiration and realization. Failing to choose quality *japa* is a choice for default *japa* (to not choose is a choice). And, of course, the result of this kind of chanting will be different.

I hope these affirmations will assist you in continued efforts to chant more purely.

Let us take inspiration from the words of
Śrīla Sanātana Gosvāmī:

"The holy name is the highest nectar. It is my very life and my only treasure."

About the Author

Mahatma Das has been serving ISKCON since 1969. He received first and second initiation in 1970 in Los Angeles, California. He has served as temple president and *saṅkīrtana* leader in several temples and has been involved in congregational development and college preaching. He was co-director of the VIHE, Krishnafest and Bhagavat Life (in the development and facilitation of *Japa Retreats*).

He now focuses on designing and conducting professionally organized workshops and retreats, both live and online, to assist devotees and non-devotees in their spiritual growth, through his company Sattva (visit www.mahatmadas.com and https://martinsattva.wixsite.com/sattva). He also counsels devotees and non-devotees, travels half the year, and writes books. He posts a daily video on his Facebook page; these videos have been so much appreciated that he has launched a separate YouTube channel named Daily Quotes by His Grace Mahatma Prabhu. He accepted the service of initiating spiritual master in 2013.

Mahatma Das is well known for his beautiful *bhajans* and *kirtans*, both live and recorded (especially for his recording of the *Brahma-Saṁhita*) and is most appreciated for helping devotees practically apply Kṛṣṇa consciousness in their lives. He presently resides in both Alachua, Florida and Māyāpur, India with his wife Jāhnavā and their daughter Śyāma-maṇḍalī.

He does several online courses weekly on Facebook, and these courses are housed on his YouTube channel and on Soundcloud (you can link to these and his other sites from mahatmadas.com and also sign up there to receive online class notifications). You can also order his books and sign up for online courses on his website.

To connect with Mahatma Das, visit:

mahatmadas.com
facebook.com/HGMahatmaDas
twitter.com/mahatmadas
youtube.com/user/Mahatmadasa
soundcloud.com/mahatma-das

You can also receive daily inspirational quotes
by Mahatma Das on WhatsApp.
Send a request to +52 15535020952

Acknowledgements

My sincere thanks would go to:

Gaurangi Gopi Devi Dasi
– transcription –

Sonal Mathur
– editing –

Vignanasana Govinda Das
– proofreading –

Ashalata Icchamati
– design and layout –

Paintings by Annapurna Devi Dasi

Links

Homepage
www.mahatmadas.com

WhatsApp Group
Send a WhatsApp request to +52 15535020952

Online Class Subscription
https://bhaktieducation.teachable.com

Newsletter/ Illuminations Subscription
www.mahatmadas.com

youtube.com
www.youtube.com/MahatmaDasa

facebook.com
www.facebook.com/HGMahatmaDas

My Notes

My Notes

My Notes

Made in the USA
Las Vegas, NV
25 November 2023

81470005R00042